ANCESTORS STILL SINGING

ZEN POETRY

VOLUME 1

ROSHI BIRD

Zen Poetry
Volume I
Ancestors Still Singing

Copyright © 2021

by Roshi Bird

ISBN 978-0-9846962-1-5

Cover painting by Roshi Bird
Cover Design by Miguel De Lara
Printed in the United States of America

"Bird's evocative poetry says it all. Each poem takes you on a journey, proving that the two rules of making music apply to all works of art.

Less is more and *When in doubt, leave it out.*

Shakespeare knew that when he had Polonious advise Hamlet—*Brevity is the soul of wit.*"

~ David Amram, composer, conductor & multi-instrumentalist; author of *Offbeat: Collaborating with Kerouac*

Thank you…

My wonderful loving families, my parents and grandparents, all kindred lineage, the guidance and protection of my ancestors, Zen philosophy, the practice of yoga and meditation, the light and dark, the bright days and the dark nights, the dark days and the light nights, the inbetween, and of course, the beginner's mind.

David Amram, Rex Butters, Miguel De Lara, Annie Elizabeth Porter, Phillip Wilson, River Sanctuary Press. The city of Los Angeles, the United States of America, my Toyota Camry, the freeways, city streets, mountains & back roads and the open sky. All the love, hospitality and kindness shown to me on the road by strangers, friends, guardian angels and everyone and everything in between.

Of course, Mother Earth, Holy Gaia, for always taking care of me.

This series of Zen poetry is dedicated
to the courageous wandering visionary,
the mystic, the meditator, the pure, the
spiritual and the material, the sublime
and the ridiculous…

Also, the holy spirit inside YOU, that
thing, that creative spark that keeps
the light on.

May this collection of Zen poetry
help to wake up the shining spirit
inside each of us and illuminate, excite
and humor us into the divine, the
transcendent, the beautiful, the simple
and the pure.

May all beings be happy and free.

*Why do you stay in prison when the
door is so wide open?*
~Rumi

silence
deep silence
winters gift

the cat shakes
first snow
off her back

record breaking winter storms
christmas lights
still shine bright

what is your original nature, temple cat?

the very long night
finally
my warm bed

new years day
cold and chilly
heavy on the mind

new years eve
ghetto gunshots
happy new year

happy party, fun gathering
the shape
of the departed guests
still
in the empty room

winter wanes
spring peeks, under construction
winter rains persist
cold quiet house
my idle thoughts wild

loud city yoga studio
silent meditation
still to-do lists
i smile
and calm down
and say thanks
for being here

i waited and stirred
my blind love
jilted for winter

long desert summer
here come
the autumn smells

santa ana
hot haunted winds
suddenly bangs shut
our inner city
windows

candlelit altar
the spider
still and silent
5 times its shadow

old friends
return
in our dreams

daddy longlegs
gather on the corners
of my bed

he used to be in insurance
now a junkie
for art
and grass

zen priest
attacked
by licking dog

clean shoes
off
in front of the temple

past lives
following
behind me
on the road
yet
staying in the present

used and abused
christmas trees
strewn in the streets

side by side
the lovers
with their laptops

suddenly
the smell of summer
another time ago

empty house
spiders party

bitter winter night
swimming pool
sits abandoned

weird thoughts
written in pencil
in the library pages

cement laid fresh
still soft
cat walks through

banned book week
i go
crazy

sitting ovation
the poets
together
and proud

in their apartment
boxes
boxing
time
memories
combs and frames
moving
the families around
the blocks
and streets
finally finding
home again

neighbor
drunk
arguing
with
ghosts

City of angels
The sunsets
Heavenly

heavy rain drenches
farmers flimsy tents
at the rain or shine market

candle final embers
flickering wildly
on the buddha and tara statues

City of angels
traffic jam
from hell

walking lovers laughing
fireflies playing wildly
first summer night

beloved friend
timeless talk
long ago in summer
the conversation still alive

young wine and fresh nuts
spring blooms
the lovers unite

the crickets, the cats
the gravekeepers
keep my ancestors singing

the cheap tent
with its gaping holes
gives us a star studded night

frog on a rock
waiting
for sunset dinner date

jump purr sleep chase sleep eat out
cats first spring fight

bed too small
but perfect for
afternoon nap

heavy thunder pours
torrential
peeking first spring
sunshine
ice cream truck bell
ripples streets
awakens and smiles

day at the library
heaven in information
homeless woman snores

first summer walk
buzzing fireflies excited
stray cat accompanies
us

night light
lights up
the altar
shapes of animals
rocks
crystals
clocks
time
to wake up

friend stays over
sleeps in the guestroom
wow, intense stuff

desert drought
birds singing
fireflies frolicking

full summer
moon shadows
reflect buddha
statues shapes

one man's moon
is
another woman's sunshine

note on door:
Meditating
thank you for
leaving me alone
and giving me
my space.
namaste m.f.

long
early
morning meditation
restroom break
damn
out of toilet paper

empty winter moon
lights up
early summer plans

deep inner city
homeless alcohol poverty
temple bells
ring for
satsung

rush hour
inner city
temple bell
sings
'its time'

moon casts
impermanence
upon
sangha's
evening
zazen

homeless
alcoholics
sneak
into the temple

old sages argue
over toilet seats

full moon
brilliance
brings zen student
to illumination
'dont be fooled
by ego'
said the teacher

new years temple bells
ghetto gunshots fire
happy new year

watching my body
after death
transparent walls
just go girl,
just do it

squalid alleys
mid-city
cats
well fed

moonshadows
reflect
goddess statue

what is deepest
inner nature,
knowing,
temple cat?

old soldiers
war stories
but worst of all
was going home

natures gift:
peace

old sages arguing
over dirty dishes
and kitchen duties

homeless
alcoholics
wave
to the temple porch
non-attachment

ascetic
sits
quietly
at the computer
with headphones
and smiles

new pillows
white and soft
introduce themselves
with a neckache

stark naked
out of the bath
quick check the windows
cat ignores me

old men
stuck in new age
playing cards

houseplant vines
run the walls
cat
runs the house

only
if you plant them
will you see
the seeds
grow

full spring super moon
lights up
ghetto palm trees

the moon reflects
naturally
into the ocean:
a beautiful
unarranged marriage

from the womb
soon
we are gone

death visits in a dream:
'why do you come?'
'none of your business'
'just wake up'

late night reading
excites the brain
but she rolls over
and sleeps deeply

wild weekend in the city
ladies dress up
and dance
girls night out

far away
we are
continents divide
yet
you and i
still together

another desert drought
yet
our abundant streams
still flow

don't pick it
let it bloom
and grow:
a rose bud

she passed away
many spring moons ago
today
she was in the room with me

another hard night
working retail
exhausted, broke
she is best dressed

bartender smiles
says ok and flirts a little
steady flow
giggling girls
always left wondering

all of a sudden:
more fun
sweet smells
laughter seeps
everywhere
blazing yellow sun
ahhh, spring

birds up early
singing sweetly
spring is here!

long cold winter
old house
sprawling hallway
banister
feels warm
glints brightly
in the morning sun
spring is finally here!

old friends
long ago departed
still here

painting
with
the women of the streets
they
teach me
alot

haircut day
old hair
swept away
forever

girls on the beach
dream
of swimming
and floating
in paradise

years of wanderlust
one night
a comfortable couch

he wears
diamonds, rubies
mercedes
but no Uhaul
follows his hearse

street hooligans
cross the street
avoiding me
pit bull at the end of a leash
walks me home

strangers ceiling
the white heavens
soon
we are on our way

karate class
monks
get their asses kicked

martial arts class
the monks
kick
some serious ass

many years a gypsy
two weeks
a clean comfortable bed

years of wanderlust
one night
lasts forever

motels roof
night creatures crawl
it's their house

my thoughts
reflected in the mirror
ouch

City of angels
ocean views
heavenly

tijuana restaurant
mexicans kindly
help the white people

inner city gas station
muddy puddle sludge
green brown black
in the middle
i look down
into it
do not see my reflection,
thankfully

early morning meditation
my mind
the bright mirror

on death bed
through the window
flowers bloom
wildly

mirror mirror on the dash
please release me from the past
windshield windshield
thank you for keeping me in the present

cat sits in window
wonders when
his human slaves
go back to work

pandemic halloween
neighborhood party
only the parents
wore masks

ask the way out
of samsara
birth death cycle
before it's time to go

the little flowing stream
thinks not
of its roaring river connection

just one world
for now
another world
many worlds
soon to come

why wait?
get enlightened now
while we're
still here

autumn harvest moon
reminds
the earth
to give freely
and to share abundantly

winter moon
reminds
the cold cabins
on the lake
about spring

summer crescent
reminds
the desert tourists
to travel light

city of angels
met my demons
got to know them
dumped them
and moved on

bird perches
happily
alert
on the temple bells

just out of the temple
monks exchange
business cards

patriarchy is a
concentration camp

on death bed
birds come closer
to the window
sing louder

old monks
sit in the kitchen
afternoon conversation:
'what time is it?'

winter mice rendezvous
via
the broken oven

community garden
meeting
yes,
changing the world
creating growth

eyes
on the road
desert mirage
ahead
please blink
slow down
and
please breathe deep
keep moving
freely

light the candles
the celebration
is here

summer days hang
ah,
mother natures gift

breasts shrink
in piercing cold

night
lights up
our lovemaking
eternal

green shoots
sprout
from the ground
tiny leaves

summer days
linger
like love

my footprints
in the sand
carrying
many ancestors

the fleeting
moment
eternal

lighting flashes
satori

tombstones
still
in stark silence
prayers overheard

bare branch
small hummingbird
enjoys moments rest

other peoples
conversations
ugh
torture

LA, land of pretty people
at a summer festival
not one beautiful face

birds spring singing
sweet beautiful songs
carries spirits
right out of this world

in the horses mouth:
no gifts

birds fly
reluctantly
south

zen cat
curled in a ball
sleeps peacefully
while soul travelling

the weeds
grow tall
around our house
silent effective
alarm system

life on the road
just passing through
sharing stories and food

these are the streets
and places
where we walk
and dream

tough wrinkled hands
wrapped
in prayer beads

the farm hands
break
cheers
to
full moon
ceremony

another wild night in the city
morning after
in the mirror
plucking
a thick gray hair

on death bed
cat still cuddles
next to
my heart

everything-ness
but no me
no others
huge vast sky
oneness

being nobody,
going nowhere
peace

a frozen field
once an indigenous village
still howls

spring days
linger
like paradise

4:15 meditation
for balance and protection
damn i missed it
ill hit it tomorrow
hopefully
we make it
all together

the sounds begin
these birds
ancestor spirits singing
we chirp in the sun
and shower
these starry nights
the calm seas
the constellations
saying
this way
and
you are the lion
and thanks to the stars
and our ancestors for guiding us

About the Author

Roshi Bird has been writing spiritual, inspirational, yogic and Zen poetry for many years.

She combines her writing into poetry, humor and memoir to tell the stories of the modern yet timeless earthly (and beyond) experience.

ompoem@protonmail.com

www.ingramcontent.com/pod-product-compliance
Lightning Source LLC
Chambersburg PA
CBHW070036260626
47159CB00005B/2054